3701194434

That'd be Telling!

That'd be Telling!

Compiled by
Michael Rosen and Joan Griffiths

CAMBRIDGE UNIVERSITY PRESS
Cambridge
New York   New Rochelle
Melbourne   Sydney

Contents

British
Isles

Londo

West Indies

AFRICA

Ghana

Pakistan →

China

Egypt

India

Bangladesh →

Hong Kong

Australia

TRICKS

The Crocodile and the Monkey

told by Surya Kumari

The Crocodile and the Monkey is a traditional story from India. We talk about India as one country but really it is quite a few different countries. All over India people speak different languages. In the Punjab, people speak Punjabi; in Gujerat, people speak Gujerati; and in some parts of Southern India people speak Tamil.

Religion is very important to many Indian people. This does not only mean that they go to a temple or a mosque, it affects their whole way of life – like what they eat, what they wear, how they think, how they behave with their family, and so on.

There are many children living in Britain today whose parents or grandparents have come from India. Many Indian people also went to live in Trinidad and Guyana in the Caribbean, and Kenya, Tanzania and Uganda in Africa. Some Asian people living in Britain came from these countries.

There are many things in Britain we have India to thank for – all kinds of spices in our food, our numbers which were invented by Indian scholars, and some of our words like *bungalow* and *pyjamas*.

There was a plum tree on the bank of a big river. A monkey lived in the tree. There were crocodiles living in the river. While eating the plums, the monkey used to drop a lot of fruit onto the bank. One of the crocodiles began to

1

eat this fruit and slowly made friends with the monkey.
They became such good friends that the crocodile spent
days chatting with the monkey. He forgot all about his
wife, children and home. So one day the wife crocodile sent
the children to see what the husband was up to . . .

The children found their daddy crocodile happily
chatting away with the monkey and eating the fruit the
monkey dropped under the tree.

The wife crocodile was furious and decided to get rid of
the monkey once and for all. She sent her children to fetch
their daddy home, telling him that their mother was dying.
The daddy crocodile rushed home. As he came near, the
mother crocodile quickly lay down moaning and pretended
to be dying. The daddy crocodile was panic stricken.
He decided to rush out to get a doctor but the wife stopped
him by saying: 'I have already seen a doctor and he said I
should eat the heart of a monkey to get better.'

The daddy crocodile said: 'I don't know where to get a
monkey's heart.'

'How about your monkey friend's heart?' asked the wife.
The daddy was shocked. He said, 'I cannot kill my friend.'
And the mother crocodile threw a fit. 'You don't mind my
dying but you certainly care if your friend dies.' Then she
began to cry.

In the end the daddy crocodile had to give in because he
did love his wife. Then the wife planned a dinner and sent
her husband to invite the monkey. She wanted to kill the
monkey at the dinner. The daddy crocodile with a heavy
heart came back to the bank. The monkey welcomed him
and asked how the crocodile's family was. The crocodile
said, 'My wife was very sick but now she is better.

To celebrate this, we are having a dinner party.' Then he invited the monkey. The monkey thought he could not come because crocodiles live in the water and monkeys live on land.

'It is not possible,' said the monkey. But the crocodile put his mind at rest by saying, 'I can easily carry you on my back. My family is looking forward to meeting you.' In the end the monkey agreed to climb on the crocodile's back and so they began to travel very fast.

The crocodile was a fast swimmer. They were in the middle of the deep river when the crocodile couldn't contain himself and had to tell the monkey the truth. 'I am sorry, my monkey friend, I'm not taking you to dinner. I am going to kill you because my wife's sickness can only be cured by eating a monkey's heart. I know no other monkey but you. I am going to kill you so I can take your heart to my wife. I hope you will forgive me.'

The monkey had to think fast. He quickly said: 'What a shame you didn't tell me about this before I left the bank. I left my heart hanging on a branch before I left. Well, nothing is lost even now. Take me back quickly. I shall fetch my heart and we shall both return.'

The crocodile agreed and raced to the bank. When they got there, the monkey hopped off the back of the crocodile, and up the branches.

He shouted down from the tree: 'Dear crocodile friend, for the sake of saving your wife's life you lied and tricked me into going with you. For the sake of saving my own life I've lied and tricked you into bringing me back. Hah, my heart is safe in my body and not hanging on a branch.'
So saying the monkey hopped away from tree to tree to live

elsewhere. The crocodile returned to his family.

So, if you ever get into trouble, don't lose your wits, your hope and your heart, but use your head and find a crafty way out.

The Brahmin, the Tiger and the Fox

A traditional Indian story retold by Surya Kumari

Once, a Brahmin priest was walking in a forest to go to a nearby town, when he came upon a tiger trapped in a cage.

The tiger called out to him to stop, and begged him to lift the trap-door of the cage and free him. The Brahmin took pity, seeing a huge animal like a tiger being made so quiet and helpless in a cage. He forgot for a moment what a fierce animal a tiger usually is.

The Brahmin lifted the trap-door and let the tiger free. 'Thank you,' said the tiger. The kind Brahmin felt pleased and was about to go on his way; but the tiger had been in the cage all night long and was hungry. Once it came outside the cage, it stopped being humble and helpless. The tiger became a real tiger.

'Stop!' the tiger said to the Brahmin. 'I am hungry – desperately hungry. Let me eat you for a meal.'

The Brahmin acted fast. He didn't wait to argue. He saw a tree nearby and made for it as fast as he could and clambered up the tree as high as possible.

The tiger didn't expect the Brahmin to act that fast. It felt cross and disappointed that the meal had slipped from under its very nose. The tiger clawed and purred and

4

roared, standing at the trunk of the tree. It couldn't clamber up the tree, because it was too heavy.

A fox was passing by and wondered what the racket was all about. The tiger explained that it was hungry and would like to eat the Brahmin.

The Brahmin shouted down to the fox saying, 'It is not fair to eat me when I have just rescued the tiger from the cage. Fox, can't you make tiger see this?'

The fox laughed, though the Brahmin and the tiger didn't think it was a laughing matter.

The fox said, 'For the life of me I can't imagine a timid Brahmin rescuing a fierce tiger from a cage. I've got to see it to believe it.'

The tiger agreed to show how it all happened. The tiger walked back to the cage. The trap-door fell shut again. The tiger was in the cage. So the Brahmin came down the tree.

The Brahmin learnt that he should be wise as well as kind. The tiger learnt that he shouldn't stretch his luck too far.

Dress Factory

told by Mahbubar Rahman

Mahbubar Rahman was 13 when he wrote this story. His parents came from Bangladesh. They now live in Whitechapel in London.

Bangladesh is a new country. It was named Bangladesh in 1971. Of course, people have been living on the land that is now Bangladesh for thousands of years and Bengali people are very proud of their music, dance, poetry and stories that go back a long time in history.

Bangladesh has many rivers running through it and the

Bengalis catch the fresh fish that live in these rivers to eat. Bengalis who come to Britain sometimes say that they miss the taste of fresh fish from rivers. They cannot understand why British people seem to eat fish that isn't fresh!

Most people from Bangladesh are Muslims. Many of them who live in London are in an area called Whitechapel, where they work in factories and workshops that make clothes.

Alal and Abdul work with their father and mother. They live at 88 Settles Street. They make ladies' dresses. They have a dress factory of their own. Alal's father works very hard and he wants his sons to work hard too. Alal is 17 years old and Abdul is 19 years old. They don't want to work hard and when they don't work hard their father gets angry with them. Alal is a good tailor. He wants to make smart clothes for himself. Sometimes he makes shirts and trousers for himself.

One day Alal wants to make a jacket for himself. He goes to the market and buys jacket cloth. He goes back to his home and cuts it. Then he hides it behind some green dresses because he doesn't want his father to see it.

Alal is making the jacket today because he is going to a party this evening. He wants to wear the jacket at the party. Alal's father is at the door. He is looking at Alal.

'Alal,' his father says.

'Yes, Dad,' says Alal. He puts the jacket under the table.

'What are you doing, Alal?'

'I am machining, Dad,' says Alal.

'What are you machining?' asks Alal's father.

'I am machining the green dresses,' says Alal.

'I can't see the green dresses,' says Alal's father.

'Brr! brr! brr! brr!' the telephone is ringing. Alal's father goes out.

'Whew!' says Alal. 'That was very close. I think the jacket will be ready for the party.'

Then Alal finishes his machining and is making the buttonholes and sewing on the buttons. His father comes in. Alal puts a green dress on top of the jacket.

'Alal,' says his father.

'Yes, Dad,' says Alal.

'What are you doing?' asks his father.

'I'm making buttonholes, Dad,' says Alal.

'These dresses don't have buttonholes, Alal.'

'I am not making buttonholes, I am sewing on buttons,' says Alal.

'Then why . . .?'

Abdul comes in and says, 'There is a man at the door, Dad. He wants to see you.' Alal's father goes out.

'Whew!' says Alal. 'That was very, very close. The jacket will be ready for the party now.'

Now the jacket is ready and Alal is pressing it. He is talking to Abdul.

'Look at my jacket. It's ready for the party this evening. I made it today.'

'Alal,' says Alal's father. He is standing at the door.

'Oh! Yes, Dad,' says Alal.

'What are you doing, Alal?'

'I am pressing, Dad.'

'What are you pressing, Alal?'

'I'm pressing a dress, Dad.'

'The dresses are green, not purple.'

'Well, I'm pressing my jacket, Dad. You see, Dad, I'm

going to a party this evening.'

'A party! You are not going to a party this evening, Alal. When you don't work in the day, you've got to work all evening.'

Poor Alal!
Alal is not going to the party. But his jacket is. Alal gives it to Abdul and Abdul is wearing it to the party.

Beating the Tree

told by Ken Ma

Beating the Tree is a traditional story from China. Most people find it impossible to imagine a country that has so many people as China – there are 1000 million – that's 20 times more than in Britain.

Even though there are so many people living there and even though China has a great history of brilliant inventors, artists, engineers and scholars, many people in Britain are not very interested in China. Some people say that for hundreds of years China has been like a huge island, with the people keeping themselves to themselves – living with their own kind of writing and counting and learning from their own great thinkers.

There are a lot of Chinese people living in Britain. Most of them come from Hong Kong which is on the edge of China and is governed by Britain at the moment. Hong Kong is one of the smallest countries in the world but it makes an enormous number of the things we use every day. Look at your toys, your clothes and your holiday things and see if any have a label saying 'Made in Hong Kong' on them.

Hong Kong Chinese people speak and write Cantonese. You can see sometimes how Cantonese is written by looking on the menus in Chinese restaurants.

Little Ping sells oil in the market. One day, he gets twenty coins. He is very pleased with himself. But he has also worked very hard, and he is now tired. So he finds himself a big shady tree, puts down the oil can, curls himself up, and goes to sleep underneath it. After the time it takes to burn a candle, he suddenly wakes up to find that his money is gone. He is very upset and starts to cry.

A wise man passing by hears him crying and asks him, 'Why are you crying, Little Ping?'

Little Ping tells him that he has lost all the twenty coins he made from selling oil.

The wise man says, 'I know who has stolen your money – it is the big tree you slept under!'

The wise man fetches a stick and starts to hit the tree so that it will hand back the money to Little Ping.

When the people in the market hear that the wise man is beating the tree, they all gather round to watch. They think it is funny, and they all laugh. The wise man gets very angry and shouts at them: 'You have all been watching me hit the tree. You must pay me two coins each before you can go.'

Everybody stops laughing right away, and takes out two coins. There is nothing else they can do. Apart from being very wise, the wise man is also bigger and stronger than any of them. He brings out a pot of water and tells everybody to throw their money into it. One by one, they put their two coins in. But when it comes to Fat Lee's turn, the wise man suddenly says, 'You are the thief!

You have stolen Little Ping's money.'

How do you think the wise man knew that Fat Lee was the thief?

'Look at your two coins,' the wise man explains. 'They are covered in oil.'

Fat Lee cries, 'I did not steal his money!'

'Take out all your money, Fat Lee!' the wise man commands.

When Fat Lee brings out his money, sure enough, everybody can see that there are eighteen coins and they are all covered in oil. So the policeman comes and takes Fat Lee away.

As for Little Ping, he gets all his twenty coins back, and he is very happy.

What do you think happens to the money in the water?

Hypnotism

told by Michael Rosen

Michael Rosen who tells this true story about hypnotism is a writer and broadcaster. He lives in London. London is a huge city made up of many small towns. Some of the small towns are made up of small villages. So, when we talk about people being 'Londoners' you have to remember that some London villagers are very different from others.

London has been the point of arrival for millions of different kinds of people over the years: Chinese, French, Irish, Jews, Moroccans, Portuguese, Scots, Africans, Caribbeans, Indians, Welsh and many many more.

Out of this mixture of people, new buildings, ways of eating, music making, story-telling and talking have grown up. Here are some examples: Jamaican reggae music, Chinese take-away restaurants, street names like Cyprus Street, words like 'nosh' from the Jews, children calling each other 'guy' from the Caribbean, a new mosque in Regents Park, and so on.

Alongside this, traditional English ways also carry on: fish and chip shops, Cup Final day, Bonfire Night celebrations, and so on.

Quite often I like to think of the things I used to do when I was a boy. I remember once a boy came to school and said: 'I can hypnotise people. I can make them go to sleep.'

So we said, 'Yeh, yeh, I bet, I bet.'

He said, 'OK, playtime.'

So, playtime, we all went out onto the playground and he said, 'Right, who wants a go?'

So Trevor, Trevor he said, 'Yeh, me.'

So this boy made Trevor lie down on the ground on his back and took his gold ring out of his pocket and put it very carefully between his eyes, on the bridge of his nose. Then he took this conker out of his pocket. It was on a string. Then he starts swinging the conker to and fro in front of Trevor. And he goes: 'Watch the conker, watch the conker, go to sleep, go to sleep.' It went on for ages and we were all crowding round, dead quiet, watching Trevor, amazed and listening.

'Go to sleep, go to sleep.'

'Is it working?' 'Is he going to sleep?' 'Wow, he's asleep.'

Suddenly the bell went and Trevor, he just sat up, got up off the ground and dusted himself down. So we all go, 'Hey, were you asleep, were you falling asleep, Trev, were you hypnotised?'

And he looked at us and he went, 'All I got was a headache.'

Trick

told by Michael Rosen

When I was a boy, I used to share a bedroom with my brother. He was older than me, and he was always making me laugh, telling me jokes, and playing tricks on me. I remember there was a time, when he would lie on his back in bed (this was in the mornings) and then he'd lift his arms straight up in the air and he'd say, 'Aah my magic bar.' And he'd pretend to grab hold of a bar above his head. Then he'd pretend to pull on this magic bar till he was sitting up in bed. And I'd say, 'You haven't got a magic bar.'

'I have,' he'd say.

'You haven't,' I'd say.

'I don't care whether you believe me or not,' he'd say and he'd go out of the bedroom.

Then very quietly I'd get out of bed, cross over to his bed and then wave my hand about in the air where that magic bar was supposed to be.

'Aah there you are,' I'd say to myself.

I knew there was no magic bar, but if my brother had ever seen me doing that he could have called out at me: 'Aah ha ha ha – tricked you.'

A riddle from India

A farmer, a tiger and a lamb.
Once there was a farmer who reared a tiger and a lamb.
In order to go to his farm, the farmer had to cross a deep
stream on a narrow bridge of simple planks. One day he
discovered he did not have any green grass where he lived
so he went to his farm where there was plenty of it.
He took with him his two animals, the tiger and the lamb.
On his way back from the farm, he had the tiger's leash in
one hand and the lamb's in the other and his bundle of
green grass on his head. When he came to cross the stream
he found that he could take only one item at a time, but
even then he had problems. If he took the tiger first and
left the lamb and the grass behind, he knew the lamb
would eat the grass. If he took the grass and left the tiger
and the lamb behind, the tiger would eat the lamb. If he
took the lamb first and went back to get the tiger or the
grass to leave it with the lamb, then either the tiger would
eat the lamb or the lamb would eat the grass. Now, how
does the farmer take the tiger, the lamb and the grass
across the bridge?

The solution is on page 88.

Lord Jim

I knew an old bloke and his name was Lord Jim
And he had a wife who threw tomatoes at him.
Now tomatoes are juicy, they don't injure the skin,
But these ones they did. They were inside a tin.

GREEDY

Anansi and the Birthday Party

told by Alex Pascall

This Anansi story comes from the West Indies. If you look at the map you can see the islands of the West Indies in the Caribbean Sea.

The people who live in the West Indies are mostly people whose ancestors were taken there from Africa hundreds of years ago. But there are also people living there whose ancestors came from India, China, Ireland, Scotland and Spain.

Some people like to call the West Indies and the other islands in the Caribbean Sea – 'The Caribbean'. This is because the first people to live there were called Caribs.

The Caribbean people speak some different languages – English, Creole (a mixture of English and some African languages), French Creole, and Spanish.

The people of each island have different ways of talking, different ways of cooking, different ways of enjoying themselves.

People from the Caribbean have been living in Britain for 300 years. Twenty years ago many Caribbean people came to live and work in Britain. Most of them came from Jamaica, Barbados, Guyana, Montserrat, St Vincent, Dominica, St Lucia, Grenada and Trinidad.

Here are some Caribbean ways of saying things that you may hear:

'wh'appen' – people sometimes say this when they meet. It means something like 'How is it going?'
'I nyam up mi food' – 'nyam' means eat. It's a word that comes from the Fan language of Ghana.
'What we going fe buy?' – 'What are we going to buy?'
'It cool' – 'It's good' or 'It's very good'.

Alex Pascall who tells this story was born in Grenada in the Caribbean. He came to Britain when he was a young man. He's often on the radio and television because he's a musician, a story-teller and someone who likes to watch other people.

My daddy used to tell me some fantastic stories about that tricky little spider called Anansi. Just around the time in the evening when it was getting dark, daddy would look at me and he would say, 'You think you're smart? You know, you remind me of that teeny-weeny little spider.'

Well, the spider is Anansi. Anansi is sometimes a spider. Anansi is sometimes a man. And he loves birthday cakes. He loves the smell of good cooking.

Anansi knows about twenty little school boys and one of them has a mother who is baking such a beautiful cake. So Anansi decides to slip into the school and get into the bag that the boy carries. Then the boy will carry the spider home and Anansi will see that beautiful cake. He hops into little Johnny's bag and home he goes.

There he hears the boy's mummy telling her friend a secret. Mummy is giving a special surprise birthday party and she isn't going to tell Johnny about it. What she is going to do is invite all his friends, make beautiful cakes, beautiful jelly, ice-cream and everything, hide it all in a room and wait for them to come in. When Johnny is upstairs she will call him down and say: 'Johnny.'

'Yes, Mummy.'

'Come down, I want to see you.'

And she will surprise him.

But Anansi has the biggest surprise for them. He gets out of the bag and he roams about Johnny's house until he slips past the door as Johnny's mummy is closing it. He gets inside the room and, boy! all the lovely jelly and ice-cream and nuts and chips and everything, that beautiful smelling cake that Mummy was making – they just all vanish into the belly of brother Anansi.

You know what it feels like, when your tummy is heavy. So Anansi has a sleep. Then he gets up and he eats some more. Johnny is upstairs. All his friends are now coming in

16

for the party. Anansi is sleeping.

'Bing, bong!' Out comes Johnny's mother.

'Hallo Joan, hallo Robert, hallo Philip, hallo Jane – come in, come in. Ssh, ssh, in case Johnny hears.'

She hides them in a room and she says: 'Johnny.'

'Yes, Mummy.'

'Come down, I've something for you.'

Little Johnny comes down the stairs. (Mark you, he's a tricky little guy. He was playing in the sink upstairs with his little Action Man.) He hides the Action Man, and he comes down very slowly.

'Hallo, Mummy.'

'Come Johnny.'

Mummy pushes the door open and all his friends come out. Johnny didn't know. They all sing, 'Happy birthday to you'. Oh, Johnny is feeling so good. They are feeling good too, knowing they are going to eat all that beautiful party cake and all the ice-cream. So mummy says, 'Johnny, I have got a big surprise for you.' And she says, 'One minute, one minute, let me go into the other room.'

By this time Johnny is beginning to suspect. Mummy goes into the room to light the candle. The candle has gone, the cake has gone, the jelly has gone, the chips, everything has gone. Anansi has gone.

Man, the mother doesn't know what to do. She says, 'Come on, Johnny, have a look inside there. I prepared all this for you and what's happened? It's all gone.'

Little Robert says, 'I wonder what's wrong. I wonder if it's that little spider I saw creeping around the classroom.'

Philip says it too, Harry says it and they all say it, except Johnny – he never saw the spider.

Ah, they didn't know that little spider was Anansi and

Johnny never checks his bag to go home. He doesn't check it to come to school. So everything is lost. The mother hasn't a drop of orange squash, nothing.

Anyway, they get on the piano and they play and they sing. Johnny's mother runs down the road and buys a few packets of chips and they have a beautiful evening.

At the end of the party, Anansi is away with his big belly and his hairy legs, well fed.

Well, you might want to know what the moral of that story is. The moral of the story is – before you leave home in the morning you should check your bag. You might forget your homework, but on the other hand you may not know what is in the bag, or who is in the bag. It could be that hairy monstrosity, the atrocious Anansi the Ashanti.

Goha in the Restaurant *and* Goha's Guest

told by Claudia Roden

These two stories about Goha are traditional Egyptian stories. Just saying the word 'Egypt' often reminds people of the pyramids and mummies – the life of Ancient Egypt thousands of years ago. Sometimes people forget that today Egypt is a modern country with cities, factories, cars and televisions – like most other countries in the world.

Most of the people living in Egypt today are people called Arabs. They also live in such countries as Algeria, Morocco, Tunisia and Saudi Arabia. Most Arabs follow the religion of Islam and call themselves Muslims.

When European people went to the Middle East hundreds of years ago, they learnt a great deal from the Arabs. They learnt, for example, how to build big buildings and how the blood flows round our bodies. Nowadays the Middle East is famous for different things, such as oil or, sadly, wars.

In Britain today there are people who have come from countries like Morocco and Turkey. Some English words have come from Arabic, like: lemon, sugar, orange, alcohol and sofa.

Claudia Roden, who tells these stories, teaches people how to cook Middle Eastern food. She was brought up in Egypt.

Some of you may have eaten Middle Eastern foods. You may have eaten shish or doner kebab or moussaka in a café or your mother may have bought houmous or taramasalata or pitta bread at the supermarket. And of course those of you whose mother or father has come from Cyprus have eaten this food at home.

But did you know that Middle Eastern food was even more popular in Britain in the Middle Ages – at least with lords and ladies and the people at the King and Queen's court?

I wrote a book on Middle Eastern food and if you look at very old English cookery books you will find that the food in those old books was like the food in my Middle Eastern cookery book. Most of the dishes have gone out of fashion over the centuries but some are still here – like rice pudding and marzipan, mince pies and Christmas pudding. Some sauces like mint sauce and "OK sauce" were invented in ancient Persia (now called Iran). I put proverbs and poems, songs and stories about food in my cookery book. Many stories were about a man called Goha. In Egypt nearly all tales were told about him.'

Goha in the Restaurant

One day Goha went to the market. He stopped to gaze into the window of a restaurant where some really nice tasting food was laid out – pilavs, stews, chicken, fish and other dishes.

Goha stood there enjoying the delicious smell that was coming through the open door. 'Mmmmmmmm.'

Suddenly the head cook called out to him, 'Come in, sir, and make yourself at home.' That's the usual way of bringing in customers. Goha thought he was invited as a guest. So he said, 'Yes, thank you.'

He sat down and ate as much as he could of all the dishes and then he filled his pockets with pilav to take home to his son. Then he got up to go. But the head cook called out: 'Hey you! – pay me. You have eaten 10 piastres worth of food. Come on. Pay me.'

And Goha said, 'But I haven't any money. I thought I was your guest.'

The head cook took Goha to see the Emir, the local judge. The Emir ordered Goha to ride through the streets

sitting backwards on a donkey as punishment.

As he went through the streets on the back of the donkey people in the streets jeered and shouted out at him. And some of them even played pipes and banged drums.

As all this was going on, one of Goha's friends saw him and called out: 'Hey, Goha, what are you doing? Why are they doing this to you?'

And Goha said: 'I was served good pilav for nothing, with extras thrown in for my son. And now I am having a free donkey ride with free music as well.'

Which I suppose all goes to show that things seem different, depending on how you look at them.

Goha's Guest

Another time Goha invited a friend round to *his* house. Goha put a plate piled high with food in front of his friend and the man quickly ate it all up. Goha put another plate of food down. The man ate it all up. Again and again, Goha rushed off to fetch more beans, more rice, and more chick peas. This food was what he had got ready for his own dinner and for the next day's dinner as well.

Finally there was nothing left to eat. Then this man said: 'I must go now – I'm on my way to the doctor because you see I've lost my appetite – I'm a bit off my food.'

You can imagine, Goha was horrified – so he said, 'Well, please, please, whatever you do don't come back when you get your appetite back.'

Some people don't know just how greedy they are, do they?

King Anansi

Words and music by Alex Pascall

Repeat from ★★ to end.

Instant Food

Instant food is good for you
There isn't time to make a stew,
Just add water and heat it through,
Instant food is good for you.

Instant food is here to stay,
Good for you in every way,
A different tin for every day,
Instant food is here to stay.

With frozen chips and pies and beans
Trickling out of slot machines
Chewing-gum, chocolate, peas and greens,
Frozen chips and pies and beans.

Instant food, prepared in a tick,
Open the packet, it's clean and quick,
And never you mind if it makes you sick,
Instant food, prepared in a tick.

Reply:
Instant turkey and Christmas pud,
Instant food it ain't no good,
It looks like plastic and tastes like wood,
Instant turkey and Christmas pud.

Instant food is just a bore,
At heart I'm just a carnivore,
Give me the meat, all bloody and raw,
I'll throw the bones all over the floor,
And then I'll come back and I'll ask for more.
Instant food is just a bore.

Miles Wootton

Two little sausages
frying in the pan
one went pop
and the other went bang.

Jelly on the plate
Jelly on the plate
Wibbly wobbly wibbly wobbly
Jelly on the plate.

Sausage on the floor
Sausage on the floor
Pick it up pick it up
Sausage on the floor.

CHASES

The Cat and the Mouse

told by Felix Cobbson

Felix Cobbson is a musician and story-teller from Ghana.
Ghana is a country in West Africa. Its capital city is called
Accra. It has big buildings, streets jammed with cars and
buses, factories full of people working just like other big cities
in the world. There are also farms and big forests in Ghana.

Some people in Ghana speak English, and many people
speak Twi and many speak Fan. Ghana is the home of
Anansi stories. The Ashanti people made up these stories
and they still tell them today.

Three hundred years ago, many farmers and miners and
people who made things out of gold were taken from Ghana
to the Caribbean. This is why Anansi stories are told in the
Caribbean.

Today there are Caribbean people in Britain who tell Anansi
stories (for example, Alex Pascall's story) and also Ghanaian
people who tell Anansi stories. Some of the stories have
made a journey from Ghana to the Caribbean and then to
Britain; some have made the journey straight to Britain from
Ghana.

The Cat and the Mouse is also a traditional story from
Ghana.

Hundreds and hundreds of years ago there lived the cat
and the mouse. Now I'm going to tell you why the cat
doesn't like the mouse.

The cat and the mouse were the best of friends, hundreds and hundreds of years ago in Ghana, in West Africa. They did everything together. They went out shopping together. They even went to discos together.

And then one day the cat said to the mouse, 'I have a brilliant idea. Let's have a party and invite all our friends to the party.'

The mouse said, 'What a brilliant idea – a party! Plenty of food – yum, yum!'

Then the mouse said, 'What are we going to do?'

So the cat said, 'We'll cook the best meal for our friends, for our guests, for everybody in the village.'

They decided that they were going to roast a whole calf, hundreds and hundreds of chickens, fish, big yams, mountains of all the yum yum that you can think about.

So the date was fixed. Then they started the preparation. It took them five days to get the food ready. The whole community knew about this big party which was going to be given by the cat and the mouse. As it was a big occasion, all the villagers came in with their drums and their best robes. It was a sight worth seeing.

And then what happened?

The mouse said to the cat, 'Oh yes, I remember when my forefathers had a party, they went to the farm for some fruits for the guests. So let's go to the farm and bring all the fruits we can think of, so that at the end of the party we can ask our guests to help themselves.'

The cat said, 'What a brilliant idea.'

So tick-tock, tick-tock, they set off for the farm. Just as they were about to arrive at the farm the mouse said, 'Oh dear, oh dear. I've forgotten my pipe, so I've got to go back home for my pipe.'

And the cat said, 'Oh no, come Mousey, we will go to the farm first and help ourselves to the fruit.'

And the mouse said, 'No, no, no! I can't work on the farm without my pipe. I've got to smoke.'

So the cat allowed the mouse to go back home for his pipe. And when the mouse got to the house, the smell of the roasted pig, all the yummies displayed on the table . . . the mouse couldn't help himself. Straight away he jumped up onto the edge of the big pot and started eating. He ate and he ate until he ate up practically everything. Now his stomach became so big that his weight tilted the pot and covered him up.

'Help, help!'

There was no-one there to help the mouse.

Meanwhile the cat waited and waited for the mouse, and then he decided that he would go back home.

When the cat got back, he cried: 'Mousey, where are you?' The mouse was nowhere to be seen.

The cat ran to the dining room.

'What – everything is eaten! Not a single drop of food!'

So the cat started searching for the mouse. He went round looking for the mouse. Then, all of a sudden, the cat heard some strange noises, scratching noises.

'Who is there?'

'Help, help!'

The cat got hold of the pot and lifted it up. And what did he find under the pot? Who can tell me?

The mouse.

As soon as the mouse saw the cat, then he started running, up the stairs, down again, behind the wardrobe, through the kitchen, behind the sink, up the drainpipe, down again, into the garden, inside again, out. The cat started chasing the mouse all over the place. Then the mouse ran away.

After that the cat swore that as long as he lived he would get the mouse. So that is the reason why the cat doesn't like the mouse.

Now, what does this story tell us? Can anybody tell me what this story tells us?

Don't be greedy. The story tells you not to be greedy. In Africa we use stories like this to send messages to the children, to tell the children in the community not to be greedy, not to be anti-social, to have respect for their elders. All over Ghana every evening you see Grandma and Grandpa sitting with all the children around them, telling stories like this one.

The Red Rogue of the World in Three Letters

told by Michael J. Murphy

This is a traditional tale from Ireland. Ireland is an island. Once it was all one country, but today it is divided into Eire and Northern Ireland. The capital city in the south is the famous city of Dublin, and in the north it is the city of Belfast. Away from the cities, in both parts of Ireland, most people work on farms. Among these country people there are brilliant story-tellers, fiddle players, pipe players and dancers.

Once everyone in Ireland spoke Irish. Today many people still do, but nearly everyone now speaks English instead. But Irish people have their own way of speaking English. Sometimes they finish sentences with little sayings like 'to be sure', or 'indeed it is', 'it is that, so it is'.

For hundreds of years Irish people have left Ireland to live in America, Australia, and England. Here are some Irish names you may know: O'Connor, Kennedy, Kelly, Sullivan, Murphy, Docherty, Boyle.

In our school we had a master who was fond of puzzles and spellings. As soon as you could spell cat and mat and bat and men and hen and box, he'd say to you: 'Now, can you spell red rogue of the world in three letters?' The answer was FOX, and indeed old people used to talk of the cute and cunning fox and the clever fox.

Well, there was this clever fox and he roamed the hillside of Sleeve Gullion, the famous mountain of South Armagh in Ulster. The men could neither trap, snare, nor hunt him down. They were very angry, because Mr Fox, as they called him, was having fine dinners and suppers on the geese and ducks and fat hens.

There was an old man living alone in a wee cabin on Sleeve Gullion at the time. This fox had robbed him, and stolen and eaten all his hens until he had only half a dozen left. The hens were kept in a low out-house with a roof of thatched rushes. At night the fox would scratch and paw a hole in the roof, drop down onto the roost, snatch a fat hen by the legs, and get out again through the hole in the roof.

So the old man had to bring his few remaining hens into his own kitchen. He made a roost for them on the rungs of a long table at the end of the kitchen, and there they rested at night. His own kitchen door wasn't made of boards, you know. It was made instead of stout rods interlaced and woven through each other, like a basket. Doors like that were common enough at the time. Anyway, the fox couldn't get near his hens at night, and the old man thought his troubles were over. He'd forgotten that saying about the cunning and clever fox.

This day he had to go out to the town of Newry to buy a new pair of leather boots. So he built up a great fire of turf or peat clods. Now the fires in those days were on the hearth, that is on a level with the floor. That fire would be a mass of embers when he got home from the town. Outside, the clods remained firm. Inside, all was hot. One touch, and the clods fell inwards and the fire was up and ablaze.

Well, he left his hens in the kitchen, and off he went. And when he came home a few hours later, he saw that a hole had been made in the bottom of his kitchen door. The rods had been pawed and pressed apart, while inside the house his hens cackled in terror. Very well he knew

30

what had happened. Mr Fox had made that hole and was inside having a feast on one half of the remaining hens.

You can imagine how mad and furious that old man felt. He grabbed up his two new boots, and took a firm hold of the stout stick he carried. He took the hasp or catch off the door, got inside and closed it again. And, sure enough, under the table there was the fox eating one of his hens.

'Aha, Mr Fox, me laddo,' he cried, dropping his new boots to the ground at the door, 'I have you. Long runs the fox, but he's caught at last. In two minutes I'll knock you stiff on that floor, you villain.' And he dashed forward with his stick raised.

The chase started round the kitchen, from under one table and up on another, up on the old dresser. The old man was making blows at the fox, and the fox was jerking or avoiding every blow.

The hens, of course, were flying madly everywhere. Round the kitchen they went. Bowls crashed from the dresser, tin basins fell and rattled, buckets and stools were overturned. Several times the fox made a dash for the hole in the bottom of the door, but it was only just large enough to let him squeeze in. Since then he'd eaten a big fat hen. If he tried to squeeze through, the old man would be upon him with his heavy ash stick and would knock him stiff on the floor. Round the house the chase went on once more.

Well, the old man was shouting that at last he had the fox at his mercy, that his running, thieving days are over. Round the house again, but coming round past the door, with the old man at his tail, what did the wily fox do? In his mouth he snatched up one of the old man's new leather boots, and running past the hearthstone, he tossed the boot into the fire. The turf fell into the embers and up whooshed the flames and the boot began to burn.

'Ah!' The old man let out a roar at the sight of the new boot beginning to burn, and tried to snatch it out. But the flames licked round his hands, and the tongs had been knocked helter-skelter somewhere during the chase round the kitchen. By the time he found them and got his boot out of the fire, badly scorched, the fox had had time to squeeze back through that hole in the bottom of the door and away.

And, as the old man had to admit, 'Once away and still away.'

WEDDINGS

Anansi and Muzzirollinkinnah

told by Louise Bennett

Louise Bennett is one of Jamaica's favourite poets and
entertainers. She tells this story.

Did you ever hear about Bredda Anansi? He's a spider
man. He's a tricky-fy little spider man. This little Anansi,
he does all kinds of things. He gets people into trouble, he
gets them out again. He's a lovable-lovable rascal. And on
top of everything, Anansi teaches you that he's magic. The
things he does, you can't do, because he can always spin a
web and get away. But *you* can't do that. He also teaches
you that you can be hurt by your own greed or by your
stupidity – especially by your greed.

Once upon a time, there was a pretty-pretty, pretty-
pretty-pretty-pretty-pretty girl and her name was
Muzzirollinkinnah. What a name! The mother gave her
this long name because she said that when this girl gets big,
by the time she gets to be about 16, 17 or 18, people will
want to marry her. But they will have to be able to guess
her name before they marry her. Unless they can guess this
name they will never be able to marry this girl. So she gave
her this quiet name and the mother – the mother's name
was Mardy Clever – didn't make anybody else know the
name but she and the girl.

As this girl grew older, Muzzirollinkinnah was beautiful. Everybody look at her and say, 'What a pretty girl, what a pretty little girl, oh what a pretty girl.'

Lawks! all the kings of the country, mi dear, *everybody* write to Mardy Clever and say they would like to marry this pretty girl. Mardy Clever say, 'You will have to guess her name.'

Bredda Anansi decides that he's going to find out the name. Bredda Anansi went down to the riverside one day, when Mardy Clever was washing the daughter's clothes. And she washing and she singing:
'Washy mekka by yah mekka semma
Washy mekka semma mekka by yah
Washy mekka by yah mekka
semma Nancy gal
lip on de rap go ping a ling.'
She singing and she washing the clothes, mi dear.

Bredda Anansi wallow up himself inna the dirt. And when the lady turn her back to pick up another piece of clothes, Bredda Anansi walk all over the clothes and dirty up the clothes. When Mardy Clever come back, she look and she say, 'Who dirty up me daughter clothes?'

Nobody answer.

Mardy Clever vex, you know. Anyway, she take the clothes, she wash it out,
'Washy mekka by yah mekka semma
Washy mekka semma mekka by yah.'
Then she spread it out again.

As she turns her back, Bredda Anansi go and he wallow up himself worserer. Now, 'worserer' means very, very, very, very, very, very bad. In English, you have 'bad', 'worse', 'worst', but in Jamaica we have 'bad', 'worse', 'worser' and 'worserer'. Him wallow him up worserer. He dirty up the clothes. Mardy Clever vex. Mardy Clever she vex, she vex, she vex. She don't remember . . . she just say, 'Who dirty up me daughter Muzzirollinkinnah clothes?'

Anansi, head quick, Anansi catch the name. Hear Anansi: 'Muzzirollinkinnah, Muzzirollinkinnah, Muzzirollinkinnah.' He remembered the name.

Anansi run home. Anansi say he's going now to get this girl. But guess what now? Anansi didn't have any clothes or anything. So Anansi borrowed all. Some suit from somebody, and he borrowed a hat from somebody, and he borrow all kind of things. Anansi jump into a bogie. A bogie is like a little horse and carriage – but fast. He going like a big man, you know. And what's in this bogie but a fiddle? And Anansi start to sing,
'Ring ding ding, Muzzirollinkinnah
Muzzirollinkinnah, Mister Bogle a come
Ring ding ding Muzzirollinkinnah
Muzzirollinkinnah, Mister Bogle a come
Ringa dinga dinga
Ringa dinga dinga.'

Hear Mardy Clever now, because she see all the big bogie and the gentleman look so rich. Hear her:
'Oh daughter, daughter, your lover is coming,
oh daughter, daughter, your lover.'

Hear Muzzirollinkinnah:
'Mother, mother, my lover.'

Hear him, hear Anansi:
'Ring ding ding, Muzzirollinkinnah.'

Oh! Everybody glad! And you ought to see the mother and the daughter jumping up.

But, by this time she had a little brother, and the little

brother was an Old Witch Boy. An Old Witch Boy is a wizard, you know, and this little boy say to her: 'Say sister, don't marry that man. Him is Anansi, you know.'

She says, 'Go 'way, go 'way, foolish likkle boy. This is a rich gentleman. Look at him. Look at how dress-up he is. Oh no, no, no, I go marry to him.'

And hear Anansi:
'Ring ding ding Muzzirollinkinnah
Oh say, "Yes, yes".'

So Anansi married Muzzirollinkinnah and put her in the bogie. Him and her going down the road singing.

By this time now, the little brother, the wizard – remember the Old Witch Boy? – well he went underneath the bogie. He held on underneath the bogie, you see, and him gone with them. They didn't know and Anansi singing down the road,
'Ring ding ding Muzzirollinkinnah
Ringa dinga dinga.'

And she singing:
'Ringa dinga dinga
Ringa dinga dinga
Ringa ding.'

And she think she nice. Well, mi dear, while they're going, all of a sudden, the hat fly off Anansi. Hear, hear Muzzirollinkinnah: 'Husband, husband – your hat!'

Hear him: 'Make it stay, it going to the owner' and that means 'Leave it alone – it's going back to who it belongs to.'

'Make it stay – it going to the owner.'

By this time the person he borrowed it from has got his hat back. But by this Anansi had no house to take Muzzirollinkinnah to. All this time, Anansi driving along the road and looking to see if him see a big old house somewhere.

So when him reach a place, a real empty old place, a haunted looking house, Anansi stop the bogie and him jump out. By this time all the clothes that him borrow from everybody had gone back to them. So him jump up and he was . . . The Spider. And when this girl look and she saw this spider she says, 'Ooooooh!' and she scream and Anansi jump after her with him eight spider legs.

Muzzirollinkinnah screamed and she run in one corner and same time the little brother that was under the bogie, he run out from under there and cornered Anansi. Anansi run in one corner, the brother after him. He run in the other corner, the brother after. But Anansi was cornered and this brother would catch him . . .

So guess what Anansi did?

Spin a web. He spun this web. Well, that was the beginning of the spider's web. That was the first time he ever spun a web. He was so cornered. He just spins a web, quick, quick, quick right up into the ceiling so they couldn't catch him.

But from that day until today, spider spinning web and living up in house-top and is Anansi make it.

And then at the end of the story we always say,
'Jack Mandora me no choose?'
and you say,
'NONE!'
Which means that no-one in the story was any better than anybody else.

Riddles and Songs from Jamaica

told by Louise Bennett

Riddle me this
riddle me that
guess me this riddle
and perhaps not:

Jigga room
jigga hall
go inna corner
go stand up.

Solution: A BROOM

Here's a rhythm game:

Musquito one
musquito two
musquito jump in the hot callalou*

musquito one
musquito two
musquito jump in the hot callalou

I love coffee
I love tea
I love the girl
an' the girl love me

I love coffee
I love tea
I love the boy
an' the boy love me

musquito one
musquito two
musquito jump in the hot callalou
musquito one
musquito two
musquito jump in the hot callalou
BUP-see-ky-zee-ko pindar[†] shell
BUP-see-ky-zee-ko pindar shell
BUP-see-ky-zee-ko pindar shell
BUP-see-ky-zee-ko pindar shell

*callalou – a kind of spinach
† pindar – means peanut in Jamaica. It comes from the Twi language of
Ghana.

Walk Good
Walk good on your way and good duppy walk with you.
Walk good!
Walk good every day and good duppy walk with you.
Walk good!
Every day
Walk good!
On your way
Walk good!
Walk good, good follow you
If you just walk good.
Walk good!

Wedding Stories

told by Michael Rosen and Sandra Kerr

Sandra Kerr was brought up in Plaistow, in East London. She is a singer.

Mike's story

The first wedding I ever went to was my cousin's wedding and I nearly ruined it. You see, the night before the wedding – I got in quite late and I was starving hungry – so I got myself something to eat – an omelette. Now, I like garlic, I like it a lot. So I took hold of a big chunk of it, cut it up and put it in my omelette, ate the omelette and went to bed.

In the morning, the day of the wedding, when I woke up everyone was running round the house complaining about the smell.

'What is it?'

'Phoor! What a pong!'

'Where's it coming from?'

Of course – it was me. I smelt all over with garlic. I must have eaten much more than I realised. Well, everyone was furious. They were so angry. They thought I had really let them down, you know.

So we then tried to get rid of the smell of garlic off me. Of course, I had a bath, I scrubbed my teeth, I ate all kinds of things that might cover it up, or soak it up – plain bread, dry biscuits, ginger. I even put some scent on.

I put lavender water in my hair and we stopped on the way at a shop. I bought a peppermint mouth spray and all the way to my cousin's house I squirted this horrible spray into my mouth. Do you know when we got there, do you know what happened?

We rang the door-bell, my auntie Sylvia came to answer the door and the very first thing she said – the very first thing was, 'My god, you smell of garlic.' I think everyone could smell it on me right the way through the wedding. It was awful.

Sandra's story

I remember when two of my friends got married. They decided just suddenly, 'Next Saturday we'll get married'. They got the licence but of course they needed a best man. Their mate Tom used to call in on them every Saturday morning. So when he called in the next Saturday morning they said: 'Tom we're going to get married, will you come along?'

Well, Tom was a window cleaner and he had his van outside with his ladder on it and his bucket. And he said, 'Oh, yeah, alright – only I can't leave all my gear out there.' So they said, 'Leave your ladder – that's alright, that's chained onto the van, but bring your bucket in.' So they went in and they got married and there was the bride and the bridegroom, and the best man and his bucket.

Mike's story

I've got another story. It was my Uncle Ronnie's wedding. Well, it was a Jewish wedding and at Jewish weddings the couple get married underneath a kind of tent. It's a bit like the things shopkeepers pull out in front of their shops to keep the rain off. But it's very low and it's as thick as a carpet. Well, it probably gets very hot under there. Now, my Uncle Ronnie and the bride were standing under this and it was just getting to the point when they were about to put the ring on. Now my dad, he was best man and so Uncle Ronnie puts his hand out behind him to get it off my dad, my dad hands it him and Uncle Ronnie faints. He goes white, and faints. Sags at the knees. So my dad grabs him, props him up and that was how Uncle Ronnie got married – out cold.

The frog's wedding song

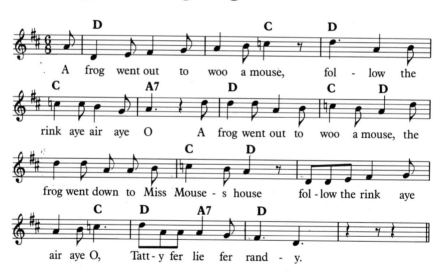

A frog went out to woo a mouse, fol - low the rink aye air aye O A frog went out to woo a mouse, the frog went down to Miss Mouse - s house fol - low the rink aye air aye O, Tatt - y fer lie fer rand - y.

2 At first he came to Miss Mouse's Hall
  There he did knock and there he did call.

3 He said, 'Missy Mouse, will you marry me?'
  'I will,' says she, 'if my uncle agrees.'

4 Consent was given and that was that,
  The wedding reception was held in a hat.

5 The first to come in was a bumble bee,
  He carried his fiddle on his knee.

6 The next to come in were two little white dogs,
  Complete with breeches and with clogs.

7 The next to come in was a big, black snail,
  He carried his bagpipes on his tail.

8 They all made merry and danced around,
  Until there was no more wine to be found.

9 The next to come in was a big black cat,
  He ate Missy Mouse and that was that.

Traditional

Tottie

Some of the words in this song from London don't quite mean
what they say.

As she walked along the street with her little plates of meat
And the summer sunshine falling on her golden Barnet
Fair,
Bright as angels from the skies were her bright blue mutton
pies
Through my east and west Dan Cupid shot a shaft and left
it there.

She'd a Grecian I suppose and of Hampstead Heath two
rows
In her sunny south they glistened like two pretty strings of
pearls
Down upon my bread and cheese did I drop and murmur,
'Please
Be my storm and strife, dear Tottie, oh you darlingest of
girls.'
Then a bow-wow by her side, who till then had stood and
tried
A Jenny Lee to banish what was on his Jonah's whale,
Give a hydrophobia bark, she cried, 'What a Noah's Ark!'
And right through my rank and riches did my cribbage
pegs assail.

Ere her bulldog I could stop, she had called a Ginger Pop,
Who said: 'What the Henry Melville do you think you're
doing there?'
And I heard as off I slunk, 'Why, the fellow's Jumbo's
trunk!'
And the Walter Joyce was Tottie's with the golden Barnet
Fair.

Traditional

Cockney rhyming slang

plates of meat	feet
Barnet Fair	hair
mutton pies	eyes
east and west	chest
I suppose	nose
Hampstead Heath	teeth
sunny south	mouth

44

bread and cheese	knees
storm and strife	wife
Jenny Lee	flea
Jonah's whale	tail
Noah's Ark	lark
rank and riches	breeches
cribbage pegs	legs
Ginger Pop	cop (policeman)
Henry Melville	the devil
Jumbo's trunk	drunk
Walter Joyce	voice

GHOSTS

The Fisherman and the Mermaid

told by Seamus Heaney

Seamus Heaney is a poet from Northern Ireland. He now
lives in Dublin.

I heard this story from a man called Sean O'Haughey in West
Donegal on the north-west coast of Ireland, a place of sea
and mountain, where the houses are whitewashed and their
roofs are covered with thatch made of straw or made of grass,
and inside the houses to this day still they burn turf, and the
fire is open and on the floor and at night the people used to sit
round those fires telling stories like this. And I'll tell you the
story as I heard it from Sean O'Haughey.

There was a fisherman in this district, one time, walking
out along the strand late in the day, when he hears this
strange singing coming from behind the rocks. So he
creeps over behind the rocks, and peeps in between them,
and what does he see but a mermaid sitting there, combing
her hair? And the next thing he spies, lying spread out
behind her, was her magic garment. Well now, if you steal
a mermaid's magic garment she has to follow you, for
there's no way she'll be able to get into the water again
without it. So doesn't the fisherman creep up behind her
and gather the garment into his arms and make off with it
down the strand as quick as lightning, nearly afraid to look
back?

Well, next thing, the singing stopped, and the fisherman stopped. But he still didn't look behind him. He walked on a bit again, and stopped again. But this time he did look behind him, and, sure enough, she had appeared out from behind the rocks and was standing there staring after him.

'Well, I have you now, my lady,' he says to himself.

And he sets off up the cliff, over the field, through the gate, across the yard, and into his house.

He was standing there for a good while in the middle of the floor examining the garment, the way it was woven of stuffs green as seaweed and blue as the sea itself and brown as wet sand, when the next thing, a shadow passes slowly by the window and darkens the door behind him. When he turns round there's the mermaid standing just inside the doorstep with her eyes wide open but looking as if she's in a kind of dream or sleepwalk, gazing round the kitchen all bewildered. It was the first time she'd ever been into a house, the first time she'd seen a fire or felt a warm floor or seen a roof over her head. And when she was standing there in her daze the fisherman slips out past her and hides the garment in the best place he could think of. And that was up under the thatch of the roof, where it would be dry and warm and well out of the way.

'Oh, where is my garment now?' she says, when he came back into the house.

'Oh, the garment's safe enough,' he said. 'As safe as it was when it was on your back in the waves of the sea.'

'If I ever see it, I will take it and be as I was before,' she says.

'If ever you see it, I suppose you will,' said the fisherman. 'But sure you'll be happy with me here until that time, and then again, that time might never come.'

So the mermaid stayed with the fisherman that night and the next night and the next night. The fisherman found land clothes for her, and in time they were married, and as the years went by they had children, boys and girls growing up around the doors, the same as other fishermen's families.

Then bit by bit the fisherman began to forget about the garment, rolled up in its warm nest under the thatch. But the mermaid herself was always wondering about it and how it had disappeared so completely since that first night. In the afternoons, as she stood at the table baking bread with her back to the warm fire, she longed to be back in the cool of the ocean floor, far away from the heat of the turf fire. And at night, when she sat in the chimney corner, the smell of the turf smoke and the smoke of the fisherman's pipe made her long for the smells of the seaweed and the tang of the sea spray. Always at the back of her mind was the memory of the magic garment.

Then, about ten years after the time the mermaid had first come to him, the fisherman sent for a thatcher to put a new roof of straw on the house. And when the thatcher landed, the first job he started was to toss off the old thatch. So, along with the forkfulls of old thatch, what does he pitch down on to the street, there and then, but the magic garment? All of a sudden the fisherman remembered, and rushed and gathered it up in his arms for the second time in his life and carried it quickly to the stackyard. Deep into the heart of the corn stack he stuffed it this time, pushed it tight in between the sheaves and came back to the thatcher well pleased with the new hiding place.

But hadn't one of the little boys been playing out on the street at the time and saw the whole performance? He ran

48

in to tell his mother about the beautiful cloth that was green as seaweed and blue as the sea and brown as the wet sand, and how his father had gathered it and stuffed it into the heart of the corn stack. And all of a sudden the old sea life stirred in the mermaid's blood, and she said to herself the words she said to him that first night: 'I'll take it, and I will be as I was before.'

Well, that night you can be sure those wide sea eyes of hers were wider open than usual, as she lay awake beside the fisherman, listening with one ear to the waves breaking in the moonlight and listening with the other ear till her husband's breathing quietened and she was certain he was in his deep night's sleep. Then out of the bed with her, all in a hurry, and quietly into the next room to take a last look at the children. And then away she flits across the street to the stackyard. She fishes in through the stack till she lays her hand on the garment. She draws it out and spreads it wide and rolls it up and folds it to her breast. She goes out the gate, and down the field and down the cliff, and across the sand, down to the rocks where he had found her singing that first evening. She shakes the garment out like a shawl and winds it around her shoulders and wades out into the moonlit foam, and as the water deepens she begins to sing again, to plunge and to play like a seal, swimming and diving all over the bay till she's too far out to be seen or heard any more.

But for years after that it was said that she left fresh fish on those rocks for the fisherman every day. And some evenings she would be heard singing away out across the water, and some nights when they were all asleep she used to creep up to home to comb the children's hair.

A Strange Stone

told by J.O. Roberts

This is a story from Anglesey. Anglesey is an island close to the coast of Wales. The gap between Wales and Anglesey is called the Menai Straits and two bridges cross there.

You can travel to the country of Wales from England without crossing a sea. You have to cross mountains though. A lot of Wales has mountains and hills where people have farms. In South Wales there are coal mines and big towns like Cardiff and Swansea.

Most people in Wales speak English but a lot of people speak Welsh too. Once, long ago, everyone in Wales spoke Welsh. If you go to Wales, one of the first things you notice is the way people speak. Sometimes you hear Welsh and

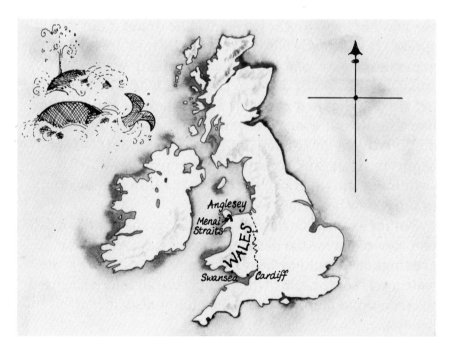

sometimes you hear English spoken in a Welsh way.
It sounds very clear and musical.

Lots of people who do not live in Wales have Welsh names.
This is because over the years people have left Wales and
gone to live in London, Birmingham, Liverpool and other
areas in England. Here are some Welsh names: Evans,
Griffiths, Morgan, Jenkins, Hughes, Rees.

Now Anglesey has many folk tales, and I'd like to tell you
one about a field – quite an ordinary field, but it became
very famous. In the old days two saints had their meeting
place at a well near this field. Where these two saints met
there's a strange stone. It has the shape of a man running,
with a bundle on his back. This stone is called the thief of
Dyfrydog. It's called the thief of Dyfrydog because, as the
story goes, the thief was running across the field with the
bundle on his back when he saw the ghost of one of the
saints and he was turned into stone. And if you lock at him
today you will see him with the bundle on his back as if
he's running.

The other reason why this field is famous is the strange
story of the daughter of Ivan Griffith. Now Ivan Griffith
was a widower and he had a daughter called Gwen. One
Christmas day Gwen had promised to go to Hafod Ucha for
what we call in Wales a Noson Lawen, a merry night.
Gwen's father told her, 'Before you go I'd like you to find
the cow. Put the cow in, and then you can go.'

So she went. But she couldn't find the cow anywhere.
She looked and she looked, but no cow. She called the
name of the cow, no response. She went back to her father
and said, 'I can't find the cow anywhere.'

'Oh,' he said, 'it's no use asking you to do anything, I'll
come with you.'

So the two of them went. They looked and they

searched, but they couldn't find the cow.

Suddenly, they heard some strange music, and it was coming from a great distance. So they went in the direction of the music, and as it grew stronger they came closer to this field I told you about. And they looked over the wall, and there, to their surprise, and Ivan Griffith couldn't believe his eyes, they saw a fairy circle and they were dancing around: little fairies with coloured dresses. They were dancing and dancing and dancing. Before her father could stop her, Gwen had joined in the circle and was dancing with these fairies. As he was about to grab hold of her, they disappeared, the fairies and Gwen. And there he was standing in the middle of the field of the thief of Dyfrydog, no-one there but the stone and himself, and he didn't know what to do.

Somebody said to him that the thing to do was to go and see the magician. This strange magician said, 'I'll tell you what to do. A year to the day, go to the same field, but first of all get a very strong rope, and then get four strong men to go with you. When the circle appears, put the rope round your middle, go into the middle and grab hold of your daughter and tell them to pull.'

A year to the day, they were waiting. And as soon as this fairy circle appeared, with the rope around his middle, he went in, got hold of Gwen and pulled her out. The fairy circle disappeared completely.

I wonder if you can guess what the question was that Gwen asked her father.

'Where's the cow?'

No-one else saw what happened, except one person – the thief – and he couldn't tell anyone what happened because he was a stone.

52

Rats come out at night

told by A.L. Lloyd

A.L. Lloyd has travelled all over the world on boats which were used to catch whales and to carry cargo.

Have you ever heard of people who have the power to get rid of rats? I don't know why it is, but they seem to have a special skill to charm the rats away, and I've heard of sailors with that power.

Many years ago, when I was a young fellow, I was working on a whaling ship called the *Southern Empress*, and we had a sister ship, the *Southern Princess*. Both the old *Empress* and *Princess* were on their way down to the Antarctic where the big whales are, but first we had to call in at Aruba, in the Dutch West Indies, for what we call bunkers, for fuel oil. There was a fellow on the *Princess* who had his good clothes for going on shore in a suitcase under his bunk – fellow named Pat Brogan. And the night before the *Princess* docked in Aruba, Brogan opened his suitcase to air his best clothes for going ashore, and he found his shirt and his trousers had been nibbled to shreds by the rats, or by *a* rat anyway.

Well, Brogan got out his razor – cut-throat razor – and he went up on the foc's'le head, and he laid the razor down on the deck, edge upward. And there sat Brogan in the moonlight to watch what happened. And out came a rat, went to the razor, rubbed its mouth along its edge, along the blade, and kissed it. And then it ran back to where it came from. And one by one, other rats crept out in the dark and each of them rubbed its mouth along that razor blade, and kissed it, and then ran back again.

Well, there were quite a few rats in the old *Southern Princess*, and it took a fair while, but at last came a rat very slow, digging her little feet in the deck as if she was trying not to get to the razor, and she was squeaking in panic all the time. At last she reached that razor, and you know, she set her head over the blade and rubbed her neck along it, and cut her own throat, and fell dead there at old Brogan's feet.

Well, Brogan didn't know it, but the Skipper was up in the wheelhouse all this time and by the light of the stars he'd been watching what was happening down there on the foc's'le head. He watched what was going on from the first rat to the last, the one that cut its throat on Brogan's razor.

Then the Skipper went down to his cabin and got out his book, and he sent a fellow down from the wheelhouse to tell Brogan to come to the Captain's cabin. He paid Brogan his wages and he ordered him to leave the ship first thing in the morning, as soon as they docked in Aruba – paid him off on the spot.

The Skipper reckoned that Brogan could have done that trick to any man on board as easy as he did it to the rat.

Mind you I didn't see this for myself, it was one of the lads off the *Southern Princess* that told me that . . .

The Ballad of Tam Lin

told by Alison McMorland

Tam Lin is an old ballad from Scotland. To get to Scotland
from England you have to travel north. Scotland is a country
with parts that are very different from each other. There are
big cities like Glasgow and Dundee, with factories and
housing estates and busy streets. But also there are
mountains and open spaces that stretch for miles and miles.
Another part of Scotland is made up of different islands and
yet another part, called the Lowlands, has rich farms.

A few people in Scotland still speak a Scots language
called Gaelic – and most Scots speak English in their own
kind of way.

In Scotland you might say, 'Ye canna do that' – which means 'you can't do that' or 'd'ye ken' – which means 'do you know', or 'you know'.

A lot of people outside Scotland have Scots names like Macmillan, McKenzie, Ferguson, Craig, McLeod, McIntosh, Stewart, Campbell. Some Scots names belong to what is called a 'clan' which is like a huge family who all share the same name.

Lady Margaret's father told her on no account was she to go to the greenwood because Tam Lin was there. Now, because he had forbidden her, this made Lady Margaret all the more determined to go. One day she was sitting sewing at the window, and as she looked at the greenwood she thought she saw something white move in the trees. Now, who or what Tam Lin was she didn't know, but perhaps that flickering of white was Tam Lin. So she kilted up her long skirts and ran away down to the greenwood.

When she got there she was amazed to see so many brown nuts on the trees, and standing on tiptoe she bent one of the trees and pulled at the nuts. As she did so, a voice from behind her said:
'Why do you pull those nuts?
And why do you bend those trees?
And why do you come to the greenwood
Without the leave of me?'

When Lady Margaret looked around she saw a handsome man leading a milk-white horse. She was a bit annoyed at his questions. Who did he think he was, talking to her like that? She said:
'I'll pull these nuts if I please
And I'll bend these trees,

And I will come to the greenwood
And ask no leave of thee.'
And with that she looked straight at him. But instead of
replying he took her by the hand, looked into her eyes and
kissed her. He kissed her again and again till Lady
Margaret felt dizzy. She closed her eyes and it felt as if the
wood was spinning around them. When she opened her
eyes and looked at him, she knew then that she loved him.
This was no ordinary man – he had bewitched her. She
asked him his name and where he came from.
'My name is Tam Lin
And I've a strange tale to tell,
For once I was a human man
In Christendom did dwell.'
And he went on to tell her how he was brought up by his
grandfather, the Earl of Roxburgh. One cold day when
they were out hunting, his horse had been frightened by
something and had thrown Tam Lin to the ground. As he
lay there, he felt a bitter north wind blow over him. It was
the Queen of the Fairies. She had wrapped her cloak
around him and carried him off to Fairyland. Tam Lin told
Lady Margaret how every seven years the fairies paid a
forfeit to the Prince of Darkness. The forfeit was always
the fairest knight in Fairyland and Tam Lin was afraid that
he was the next to be given to the Prince of Darkness. Tam
Lin was scared. Now that he loved Lady Margaret he
wanted to free himself from the Queen's power.
Lady Margaret said that she would do anything for him.
'There is one thing,' he said, 'and only you can do it.
You must be brave in the sight of all that is terrible, for the
Queen will do all in her power to terrify you.'
And he told her exactly what she had to do to win her

own true love, and he told her in a song. First he told her when to wait for him, then he told her where to wait for him, then he told her he'd be changed into three things.

Tomorrow night is Hallowe'en
When Fairy folk will ride
And if you would your true love win
At Miles Cross you must bide*, my love
At Miles Cross you must bide.

Oh, first let past the black, black steed†
And then let past the brown
But quickly run to the milk-white steed
And pull the rider down, my love
And pull the rider down.

For I'll be on that milk-white steed
And my left hand will be bare
Cocked up shall my bonnet be
Combed down shall be my hair, my hair
Combed down shall be my hair.

For they will turn me in your arms
Into a snake so large
You'll hold my head, you'll fear me not
I'll do to you no harm, my love
I'll do to you no harm.

Again they'll turn me in your arms
Into a lion bold
You'll hold my head, you'll fear me not
I'll do to you no harm, my love
I'll do to you no harm.

58

Again they'll turn me in your arms
Into the burning lead
Then throw me into the well of water
And throw me in with speed, with speed
And throw me in with speed.

And then I'll be your own true love
Turned into a naked man.
Then cover me over with your mantle green
Cry out loud, 'Oh, you're won, my love, you're won,'
Cry out, 'You're won, my love.'

Dark and gloomy was the night
And eerie was the way
As fair Margaret in her mantle green
To Miles Cross she did go, did go
To Miles Cross she did go.

And first went by the black, black steed
And then went by the brown
But quickly she ran to the milk-white steed
And pulled she the rider down, oh down
And pulled she the rider down.

So well she minded what he did say
And young Tam Lin she did win
She's covered him over with her mantle green
As blithe‡ as a bird in spring, in spring
As blithe as a bird in spring.

Have you ever wanted anything so much that you'd have
held on like Lady Margaret did?

* bide – wait
† steed – horse
‡ blithe – happy

BOASTING

The Talkative Weightlifter

told by A.N. Sattanathan

Hawkhill was a small village in the south which lay near a huge rock. Every evening the hawks came to rest on the rock and that was why the village was called Hawkhill. The people of this village were simple and poor. After they had finished working in the fields they liked to watch boxing, wrestling and weightlifting. Any strong man or fast runner, visiting the village, was always treated as an honoured guest.

One day, a weightlifter from the north came to the village and gave a display of his strength. He lifted a very big stone lying in the village square, which nobody had lifted before. All the people praised him, garlanded him, gave him many gifts, and fed him on delicacies for several days.

Now, there was a mischievous man in the village, who never did any work. He talked a lot but was very lazy.

He said to the others, 'Why are you making all this fuss over this man? This fellow has been eating meat, and rich sweets, milk and fat for several days. No wonder he is strong and big and could lift that rock. If I eat meat and chicken for six months, with plenty of sweets made in fat, I would be able to carry our Hawkhill on my shoulders.'

The simple village people were taken in by him. They

took turns in feeding him, and the fellow grew big and fat. After six months, on a festival day, the villagers gathered near Hawkhill. The man who had boasted he could carry Hawkhill was there to show off his strength. He walked with pride, throwing his arms about, slapping his chest. Six months of good eating had made a giant of him.

Standing near the rock, he shouted to the villagers, 'Come along! I am waiting.'

The villagers asked him to lift the rock. But he said, 'Come on! Lift the rock and place it on my shoulders, and I promise to carry it. Come along. Lift it up on my shoulders.'

The villagers realised that the talkative fellow had cheated them. They had fed him for nothing. He could not lift the rock at all, and he had tricked them with his boasting. Now he was asking them to lift Hawkhill and place it on his shoulders! They were so angry that all of them got together and chased the silly man out of their village.

The Big McNeill

told by Sandra Kerr

Well, I'll tell you about the Big McNeill. Actually it was my Uncle Fred who told me about the Big McNeill.

You see, once my Uncle Fred worked on a building site. On his first morning there, the foreman says to him, 'Eh, right, Fred, eh, dig us a hole over there, eh, ten by six and two foot deep.'

So Fred looks around and sees an enormous spade.

He picks it up and starts to dig. Suddenly the foreman rushes over and says, 'Put that spade down, Fred, that's the Big McNeill's – he stirs his tea up with that. If he knew you'd touched it he'd have your guts for garters.'

Fred thinks, 'Must be a pretty big bloke, this Big McNeill.'

Later in the day, the foreman asks him to mix up some concrete. So Fred finds this big concrete mixer and he starts it up, clunk, clunk. The foreman rushes up and says, 'Don't use the mixer, Fred, it belongs to the Big McNeill – he brews his tea up in that.' By this time Fred was getting a bit fed up with hearing about this Big McNeill.

The final straw comes at the end of the day when Fred's doing a bit of clearing up. He picks up a big broom to do some sweeping and the foreman shouts, 'Fred, don't touch that. That's Big McNeill's toothbrush.'

Fred thinks, 'Right.'

He throws the broom down.

'I've had enough of this,' he says. 'Who does this Big McNeill think he is? Where is he anyway?'

So the foreman says, 'Well, it's his day off actually.'

So Fred gets his address and decides to go round there and sort him out. He gets to the house. The front door's open so Fred goes in – no-one downstairs but from upstairs he can hear these thundering snores. So this is his chance. He goes up the stairs into the bedroom and there on the bed there's this enormous form covered over with a blanket. So Fred picks up a chair, pulls it up above his head and he's just going to smash it down on the snoring head, when a woman rushes up the stairs into the bedroom. She says, 'You stop that now. You stop that or I'll tell the Big McNeill. That's his baby boy.'

There's a giant made of steel
And he's called the Big McNeill.
He chews lumps of rock and gravel,
Stirs his tea up with a shovel.
   Did you ever hear
   Did you ever hear
Did you ever hear such a funny thing before?

Go-kart

told by Michael Rosen

Me and my mate Harrybo – that was his name – we made a
go-kart. Now everyone was making go-karts so we had to
make one. Now Big Tony's was terrific. Big Tony was
terrific. Actually, I didn't think Big Tony was terrific, but
Big Tony thought Big Tony was terrific because Big Tony
told us he was. What he said was, 'I am terrific' and
because Big Tony was very big no-one said, 'Big Tony you
are not terrific.' So Big Tony was terrific and Big Tony's
go-kart was terrific. And that was that.

Now when Big Tony sat on his go-kart he looked like a
real driver. He had control. When he came down a road
round our way called Moss Lane, he could steer, he could
lean, he could make the wind blow in his hair, phew!
He could make the wheels of the go-kart go prrrr! As he
came down Moss Lane he went eeeeeoww as he went past.

Oh I was jealous of Big Tony. I was afraid that I thought
that he might be – terrific – so me and Harrybo we made a
go-kart out of his old pram and some boxes and crates from
the off-licence and we nailed it up with bent nails.

But Harrybo's dad says, 'Uh-uh, you should use big metal staples,' and he gave us some. He said they were 'heavy-duty'. Wow – 'heavy-duty' – that sounded terrific.

So we then tied cord round the front cross-piece. But Harrybo's dad said, 'Uh-uh, you should use the pram handle,' and he helped us fix the pram handle to the cross-piece. He said, 'That'll give you control.' Wow – 'control' – that sounded terrific.

So Harrybo sat on the beer crate and steered and I kneeled behind. But Harrybo's dad said, 'Uh-uh, you should kneel on foam pads,' and cut two foam pads for me to kneel on. Harrybo's dad said, 'That'll help you last the course.' Wow – 'last the course' – that sounded terrific.

So, our go-kart was ready. We took it up to the top of Moss Lane. And Harrybo said, 'I'll steer' and he did. It was fantastic. It felt just like Big Tony looked. The hair in the wind – phew; the wheels – prrrrr; and so we both went eeeeeeeow.

So we took it up to the top of Moss Lane again and Harrybo said, 'I'll steer' and he did – it was amazing. The road went blurry. The hair in the wind phew; the wheels went prrrrr; and so we both went eeeeeeeeeow.

We took it up to the top of Moss Lane again. Harrybo said, 'I'll steer', so I said, 'Can I have a go?'

Harrybo said 'No.'

'Oh go on,' I said.

'No,' he said. 'You don't know how.'

'Oh go on,' I said. 'Go on Harrybo.'

'No,' he said, 'you never done it.'

'Oh go on Harrybo, come on, let me have a go. Oh go on.'

'No.'

64

'Oh go on, I mean, oh go on Harrybo.'
'Alright,' he said. 'Now look out, won't you?'
'Yeh, yeh, yeh, I know,' I said. 'I am going to be

terrific.' I thought, 'My hair phew, my wheels prrr, me eeeeeow.' And away we went.

Hair – yeh, phew, wheels – yeh, prrr, me – yeh, eeeeeeow. But halfway down Moss Lane there's Moss Close and the road curves and that's where Big Tony steers, Big Tony leans, Big Tony controls, prrrrr. I saw Moss Close coming up really fast. 'Steer,' shouts Harrybo and I yanked on the pram handle, huh, and the whole world went round once and twice and three times. My head went rolling down the road pulling me after it and the go-kart came for the ride, over and over and over until my nose and my chin and my two front teeth landed up in the grit of the gutter. Yuk.

Harrybo was crying. I breathed in and it whistled. I stuck my finger up to my tooth and it was chipped.

Harrybo said, 'Your chin's bleeding.'

I said, 'Yeh, your chin's bleeding an' all.'

'I know.'

So we walked home. He pulled the go-kart, we got to his place, he didn't say anything, nothing at all, not a word and he went in. I walked on to my place, my tooth was still whistling and my chin felt kind of wet. I told mum and she said, well, she said all kinds of things. She said, 'Your teeth'll go black and probably fall out' – one of those nice things that mums sometimes say.

Next day at school they were all asking about the crash. They all looked at my tooth and they all wanted to see the go-kart. But Harrybo said, 'You can't, 'cos my dad's chopped it up.' Wow – 'chopped up'! That sounded terrible.

When Harrybo got his racer, his brand new racing bike for Christmas, I didn't ask him for a go on it – no, no, no I didn't ask him for a go on it – I wonder why.

FOOLISH

The Yogi and the Cobra

told by Surya Kumari

There once lived a cobra inside a hedge near a town.
Children used to play on the grounds near by and
sometimes many of them walked that way to go to the
fields. The cobra was a menace and killed and injured
many people. Everyone lived in fear of the cobra. One day
a wise man, a yogi, was walking in that direction. People
warned him not to go there and when he asked why they
said, 'A cobra lives inside the hedge and it's sure to kill
you.' The yogi was not put off that easily. He walked
towards the dreaded place. Suddenly the cobra shot out,
and raised its hood to strike its deathly blow, but stopped.
The yogi stood still and calm. He didn't try to run. For a
moment the cobra wondered if the yogi really was alive.
Sure enough he was. He knelt in front of the cobra and
began to speak.

'Why do you have to kill people and injure them?
You must lead a peaceful life and let others live around
you. I shall teach you the name of the Lord, so you may
take it and live in peace.'

It was an overwhelming experience for the cobra.
It quietened down and decided to change. The yogi taught
the cobra to repeat the name of the Lord. The cobra

repeated the name of the Lord and found peace and happiness in itself.

Some wicked boys of the town got to know that the cobra had become very quiet. They began to go closer and closer, they became bolder and stroked the cobra as it lay on the rock enjoying this new peace it had found. The boys went closer and held the cobra by its neck. Even then there was not a whisper, not a wriggle as a protest. One of the boys suggested it might be fun to thrash the cobra against the rock. So the poor cobra found itself mercilessly beaten, and crawled into its hole. It dared not come out even to eat and so it became as thin as a skeleton.

A year had gone by and the yogi returned. He was absolutely sure the cobra was living happily and peacefully. To his great surprise the cobra was nowhere to be found. When he found the cobra at last, it was nearly dead. He fed the cobra with milk and honey, and revived it. Then he asked, 'How have you got like this?' The cobra whispered, 'You taught me to become very peaceful. Before I knew where I was I was dragged and beaten by the wicked boys of the town.'

The yogi was shocked. 'I told you not to kill,' he said, 'but I did not tell you to stop hissing. I didn't tell you to stop frightening wicked people away.'

So, if you are a good person that doesn't mean you shouldn't shout out if someone is trying to hurt you.

Goha and the Eggs

told by Claudia Roden

A man carried seven eggs in the pocket of his robe. He met
another man in the street and said to him: 'If you can guess
what I have in the pocket of my robe, I will give you these
eggs, and if you can tell me how many there are, I will give
you all seven.'

The other man thought for a while and said: 'I don't
understand, give me another clue.'

The man said: 'It is white with yellow in the middle.'

'Now I understand,' said the other. 'It is a white radish
that has been hollowed out and stuffed with a carrot.'

A man told this story to a group of people. When he had
finished, one of the people listening asked, 'But tell us
what was there in the pocket of his robe?'

Who do you think was the silliest in this story: the man
with something in his pocket, the man who thought he had
a stuffed radish, or the man who heard the story and still
didn't know what's white and yellow in the middle?

The Wishing Tree

told by Surya Kumari

Once a traveller was walking through a forest on his way to
a distant town. After many, many miles he felt tired and
found a shady tree to rest under.

He sat down leaning against the trunk. He was so tired

he thought, 'I wish I had a soft bed to lie upon and stretch my body on.' It so happened that the tree was a wishing tree, a tree that makes your wishes come true, called 'Kalpa Vriksha'. Even before he had finished wishing – lo – there appeared in front of him a beautiful bed, with a soft mattress and some lovely pillows.

The traveller was amazed. He leapt up, went over to the bed and lay on it. He was as comfortable as a rabbit in a burrow.

He was delighted. But soon his tired stomach cried out for food. Then the traveller whispered to himself, 'Oh how I wish I had some food and fruit.' No sooner had he said this than there appeared a table laden with most tasty-smelling food and delicious-looking fruits. The traveller jumped out of bed and began to eat like a hungry wolf.

When he had eaten, he lay upon the bed again. He was completely happy . . . well, nearly completely!

He said to himself, 'How fantastic all this is! Yet I wish I had a beautiful girl by my side to press my feet and my body and hum a tune softly in my ear to soothe my tired nerves.' And, like a flash, out of the blue, there came a most beautiful girl. She smiled, and walked gracefully towards the traveller. Her hands were like petals and her voice was like trickling honey. She began to press the tired limbs of the traveller. The traveller thought he was in a dream. 'This feels like heaven,' he thought.

Suddenly an awful thought came into his mind. 'Everything I have wished for so far has come true! Supposing I was really silly and I thought of a man-eating tiger, would it really come alive and eat me?' Suddenly a thunder-like roar was heard. A tiger shot out of nowhere, pounced on the traveller and gobbled him up!!

So, if every thing we wished for came true, then the world would not be a very safe place. We would become dangerous to other people and dangerous to ourselves.

I mean, how many times have you heard someone or other get cross and say something like 'Drop dead!'

Your baby has gone down the plug-hole

A mother was bathing her baby one night
The youngest of ten, and a tiny young mite,
The mother was poor, and the baby was thin,
Only a skeleton covered in skin.

The mother turned round for the soap off the rack,
She was but a minute, but when she turned back,
The baby was gone, and in anguish she cried,
'Oh, where is my baby?' The angels replied:

'Your baby has gone down the plug-hole,
Your baby has gone down the plug,
The poor little thing was so skinny and thin,
He should have been bathed in a jug.

Your baby is perfectly happy,
He won't need a bath any more,
Your baby has gone down the plug-hole,
Not lost, but gone before.'

The Rattlesnake

A nice young ma-wa-wan lived on a hi-wi-will;
A nice young ma-wa-wan, for I knew him we-we-well.

Refrain:
To my rattle, to my roo-rah-ree!

This nice young ma-wa-wan went out to mo-wo-wow
To see if he-we-we could make a sho-wo-wow.

He scarcely mo-wo-woed half round the fie-we-wield
Till up jumped – come a rattle, come a sna-wa-wake and
  bit him on the he-we-weel.

'Oh, pappy da-wa-wad, go tell my ga-wa-wal
That I'm going to di-wi-wie for I know I sha-wa-wall.'

'Oh, John, oh, John-wa-won, why did you go-wo-wo
Way down in the mea-we-weadow for to mow-wo-wow?'

'O Sal-wa-wal-wa-wal, why, don't you kno-wo-wow
When the grass is ri-wi-wipe it must be mo-wo-wowed.'

The young man di-wi-ied, gave up the gho-wo-wost
To Abraham's bo-wo-osom he did po-wo-ost.

Come all young me-we-wen and warning ta-wa-wake,
And don't get bi-wi-wit by a rattlesnake.

Traditional

ROUND OUR WAY

My Mother Saw a Dancing Bear

told by Charles Causley

Cornwall is the last or first county in England. It just depends which way you look at the map because it is the county that is on the western tip of England. It is the warmest part of Britain and one of the most beautiful with high cliffs plunging down to sandy beaches. Inland there is rich farmland, leading on to rugged moors.

Cornish people have made their living from mining, fishing and farming. Once it was a place where smuggling went on, while today it is a great holiday place.

Cornwall differs from every other part of England in one thing: language. It is the one part of England where a Celtic language has lasted: Cornish. Here is one to ten in Cornish: Un, Deu, Try, Peswar, Pymp, Whegh, Seyth, Eth, Naw, Dek.

If you know someone with a surname that begins with Tre– or Tri– (like Tremaine or Trelawny) it is quite likely that they have an ancestor who came from Cornwall.

In Cornish the name for nose is 'frygow' and the word for hair is 'blew'.

Along with the Cornish language there is a good tradition of story-telling, song and dance. At festival-time in some Cornish towns there are traditional celebrations and street processions that go back a thousand years or more.

Charles Causley is a poet who lives in Cornwall. Here he is telling us about one of his poems.

I come from a little town in Cornwall called Launceston where I was born and have lived all my life. My mum and dad come from there too.

My mum went to one particular little school called St Stephen's School. She used to tell me a story about that school that I've certainly never forgotten.

The headmaster of the school was rather a fierce fellow called Mr Davis. He had a beard and a cane hanging on a nail at the side of his stand-up desk. One afternoon in summer, and this must have been 80 or 90 years ago, they were all working away at their long oak and iron desks, all those children. There suddenly came a great knock on the schoolroom door. That was the one that opened on to the playground. It was a door almost big enough for a church. It had big studs all over it and a big iron latch.

Anyway, over went Mr Davis to open it, and to everybody's amazement, there in a big white-hot blaze of summer light, framed by the doorway, just like a picture, was a man. He had a coloured silk handkerchief tied round his head and a kind of flute or whistle-pipe stuck in his belt. On the ground beside him was a heavy lump of metal – 'A bit like a cannonball,' my mum used to say – with a length of very strong, very long chain attached to it. At the other end of the chain from the cannonball was, what do you think? A huge, ragged, dusty bear. A performing bear. 'Bruin,' my mother used to call him.

The children fairly gasped with surprise, I can tell you. I think the headmaster did too, but I don't suppose he showed it. Anyway, the keeper asked if the children would like to see the bear do his tricks. So out they all trooped into the playground. At a safe distance they all lined up for the performance, and the keeper began to play his whistle-pipe.

'Oh,' my mother used to say, 'that bear was a splendid creature.' It had thick fur and strong teeth and claws and great massive limbs and it did everything the keeper told it to do perfectly. It rolled and it tumbled and it marched on its hind legs up and down like one of the red-coated soldiers of those days. And it lay down and pretended to have died in battle for the Queen. It even did a kind of little dance or jig when the keeper played a particularly merry and lively tune. There was no doubt about it, the children enjoyed the show.

Yet, you know, as mother used to tell me this story 60, 70 – nearly 80 years after it had all happened, I could tell that the effect on her and all the other children was rather different from the one the keeper had intended. You see,

76

there was *something* about that bear. . . that huge, rather shabby, powerful, frightened creature, hot and filthy with dust; its feet torn by tramping the rough roads, its spirit half-broken.

You see, that bear was so far, so very far from where it might have been, from where it should have been, living naturally, wandering about in great cold northern forests, and free.

And I thought to myself, 'One day, you know, I really ought to write a poem about that,' and so I did. And I called it 'My Mother Saw a Dancing Bear'.

My Mother Saw a Dancing Bear

My mother saw a dancing bear
By the schoolyard, a day in June.
The keeper stood with chain and bar
And whistle-pipe, and played a tune.

And bruin lifted up its head
And lifted up its dusty feet,
And all the children laughed to see
It caper in the summer heat.

They watched as for the Queen it died.
They watched it march. They watched it halt.
They heard the keeper as he cried,
'Now, roly-poly! Somersault!'

And then, my mother said, there came
The keeper with a begging-cup,
The bear with burning coat of fur,
Shaming the laughter to a stop.

They paid a penny for the dance,
But what they saw was not the show;
Only, in bruin's aching eyes,
Far-distant forests, and the snow.

Keep me busy

If it's tin stacks that you like, don't come to me; And
froz-en packs they aint me cup of tea; And that bloom-in super mark-et well
lad-y you can park it, But if it's nan-as that you want just come to me. Keep me
bus-y,__ let me see your face! Shill-ing ba - nan-as,__ this here is the
place. For an-y kind of coppers there's a bunch of ripe and whoppers Keep me
bus-y, __ let me see your face, love,__ let me see your face.

Chorus
Keep me busy, let me see your face!
Shilling bananas, this here is the place,
For any kind of coppers, there's a bunch of ripe and
                                        whoppers,
But if it's 'nanas that you want just come to me.

2 If it's gimmicks that you seek, don't come to me.
For the bargain of the week, don't come to me.
Come on darling, just you try'em, you won't be forced to
buy'em,
So if it's 'nanas that you want just come to me.

3 If you need a charming staff don't come to me,
And counters mile 'n'alf and a w.c.
Pay me a friendly call, pick your fancy off the stall,
'Cos if it's 'nanas that you want, just come to me.

4 If you want a noisy shop, don't come to me,
With tills that never stop, don't come to me.
You can have some peace, my dear, if you do your
choosing here.
So if it's 'nanas that you want just come to me.

5 If you think I'm out to rob, don't come to me,
'Cos I do an honest job, well, can't you see?
And the weather wasn't made for the barrow boy's trade,
So if it's 'nanas that you want, just come to me.

Jim O'Connor

Burial ground stories

told by Michael Rosen and Sandra Kerr

Michael Rosen: You know a long time ago there was a
man who lived round our way and he said: 'When I die, I
don't want to be buried in the ground – I want to be buried
in the air.' Just to make sure he would be – while he was
still alive he built this tower, this yellow tower, and said he
wanted to be buried halfway up it.

Sandra Kerr: There's a churchyard in East India Dock Road. The first time I ever went past it was on a Sunday and I must have been about four or five, and my dad was taking me to Petticoat Lane. We passed by this churchyard and there was a grave and it had a gravestone and another piece of stone on top of the grave that was carved in the shape of the Football Association Cup, you know, that they win on cup tie day. I thought this was great, and I said to my dad, 'Here, what's that?' And he said, 'Oh, that's where West Ham United is buried.' I thought that was funny, they were playing at home yesterday and they looked OK to me. But it stuck in my mind for years after and every time I went past, and especially if I was with mates, I'd say, 'Oh, yeah, that's where West Ham is buried.'

The cat's got the measles, the measles, the measles,
The cat's got the measles,
The measles got the cat.

from Bangor, Northern Ireland

Dic dic tation
Corporation
How many buses are
In this station
One, two, three, four, five . . .

from Edinburgh, Scotland

Mickey Mouse is dead,
He died last night in bed,
He cut his throat with a five pound note,
And this is what he said,
My name is Elli, Elli, Chickerli, Chickerli,
Ompomme Susie, Willawee Whisky,
Indian Chief said How.
from Vauxhall, South London, England

Humpty Dumpty sat on the wall
Eating a bunch of bananas
Where do you think he put the skins?
Down the king's pyjamas.
from Holloway, North London

Tiddley winks old man,
Suck a lemon if you can,
If you can't suck a lemon,
Suck an old tin can.

Please miss,
Me mother miss,
I've come to tell you this, miss,
I miss, won't miss,
Be at school tomorrow, miss.

Granny in the kitchen,
Doing some stitching,
In comes a boggie man,
And chases Granny out.
from Vauxhall, South London

I had the German measles,
I had them very bad,
They wrapped me in a blanket,
And put me in a van,
The van was very bumpy,
I nearly tumbled out,
And when I got to hospital,
I heard a baby shout,
'Mama, dadda, take me home,
From this little rusty home,
I've been here for a week or two,
And Oh I want to stay with you.'
Here comes Doctor Glannister,
Sliding on a banister,
Half way down he rips his pants,
And now he's doing the cha-cha dance.

from Bangor, Northern Ireland

This is a Jamaican song that goes with a game.
A girl called Jennifer sang it. She goes to school in
Vauxhall in South London.

Go down Reonlian Road
Gal and boy
to go pick rock stone
Pick them one by one
Gal and boy
pick them two by two
Gal and boy
play we da play
Gal and boy
mash your finger don't vex

Gal and boy
one stone, two stone, three stone
the diamond stone.
Take the stone and run
Gal and boy
Mash your finger don't vex
Gal and boy
One stone, two stone, three stone,
and the diamond stone.

Solution to the riddle on page 13

1 The farmer takes the lamb across the bridge and ties it to a tree on the other side.
2 He goes back and carries the grass across to the other side.
3 He unties the lamb and carries it back.
4 He ties the lamb to a tree and carries the tiger across and ties it to a tree on the other side.
5 He goes back and unties the lamb and carries it across to the other side.

Acknowledgements

The compilers and publisher gratefully acknowledge the story-tellers for permission to reproduce their stories.
The Crocodile and the Monkey, The Brahmin, the Tiger and the Fox, The Yogi and the Cobra, The Wishing Tree copyright Surya Kumari
Dress Factory by Mahbubar Rahman from *Classrooms of Resistance* compiled by Chris Searle and published by Writers and Readers Publishing Cooperative, London 1975
Beating the Tree copyright Ken Ma
Anansi and the Birthday Party, King Anansi copyright Alex Pascall
Goha in the Restaurant, Goha's Guest, Goha and the Eggs copyright Claudia Roden
Instant Food copyright Miles Wooton
The Cat and the Mouse copyright Felix Cobbson
The Red Rogue of the World in Three Letters copyright Michael J. Murphy
Anansi and Muzzirollinkinnah copyright Louise Bennett
Wedding Story, The Big McNeill, Burial Ground Story copyright Sandra Kerr
The Fisherman and the Mermaid copyright Seamus Heaney
A Strange Stone copyright J.O. Roberts
Rats come out at Night copyright A.L. Lloyd by permission of Mrs C. Lloyd
The Ballad of Tam Lin copyright Alison McMorland
The Talkative Weightlifter from *Folk Tales from the South* by A.N. Sattanathan published by India Book House Educational Trust
My Mother saw a Dancing Bear copyright Charles Causley
Keep me Busy copyright Jim O'Connor

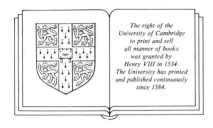

The right of the
University of Cambridge
to print and sell
all manner of books
was granted by
Henry VIII in 1534.
The University has printed
and published continuously
since 1584.

Published by the Press Syndicate of the University of Cambridge
The Pitt Building, Trumpington Street, Cambridge CB2 1RP
32 East 57th Street, New York, NY 10022, USA
10 Stamford Road, Oakleigh, Melbourne 3166, Australia

School edition first published 1985
This edition first published 1988

Printed in Great Britain by David Green Printers Limited,
Kettering, Northamptonshire

British Library cataloguing in publication data
That'd be telling!
   1. Children's literature
   I. Rosen, Michael *1946*   II. Griffiths, Joan
   808.8'99282   PZ5

ISBN 0 521 35302 5   Hardcovers
ISBN 0 521 27775 2   School edition

DS

Illustrations by Jan Nesbitt
Maps by Celia Hart
Cover by Marc Vyvyan-Jones